Snippets

Mostly True Tales from the Lighter Side of Scrapbooking

by Lain Ehmann

by Stacy Julian

Think back to when you cropped your first photo. You probably didn't realize you were taking a life-changing step by becoming a scrapbooker. You had no idea what you were committing yourself to, did you? At that moment in time, you couldn't imagine needing a dedicated space in your home for your growing collection of decorative scissors, designer papers, and colorful doodads. And I'm sure you had no indication that, by the time your first-born hit age 15, you'd be willing to send him packing so you (and your crafting supplies) could take over his bedroom!

Yes, the scrapbooking mindset is a strange and wonderful place, and I've been immersed in it for a long time. Long enough to be horrified that I've invested more money in patterned paper than in my 401(k). And long enough to realize how essential it is that we infuse our creative pursuits with playfulness—that we laugh at ourselves and all of our idiosyncrasies. And I can't think of anyone better suited to encourage this self-effacing humor than Lain Ehmann.

I became acquainted with Lain years ago when she sent me a handful of her humorous observations about scrapbooking. The first time I read them, I was traveling to a soccer game, reading and drinking a soda, and doing the laugh-and-snort thing from the passenger seat. "Listen to this..." I said repeatedly to my husband, reading excerpts of Lain's delightful, lighthearted essays aloud.

Lain has a gift for poking gentle fun at the quirky things we do in our quest for perfect scrapbooks— for capturing the comical in the everyday life of a memory-preserving female. Being just such a female, I am thrilled to introduce Lain, and her amusing snippets, to you.

Enjoy! But don't try to drink soda while you read. It's not a good idea.

Stacy Julian
Founding Editor, *Simple Scrapbooks* magazine

{ DEDICATION }

To my children—Ben, Kinsey, and Callie.
You represent the very best part of me.

And to John, who is the reason for it all.

{ ACKNOWLEDGMENTS }

"Thanks a lot" doesn't begin to cover it, so let's try "merci beaucoup," which means the same thing but makes me sound more sophisticated.

...to Ben, Kinsey, and Callie, who give me plenty of material on a daily basis.

...to John, who has never complained (at least audibly) about the stacks of pictures and paper all over the house.

...to my parents, Bill and Judy Chroust, for letting me take over as family historian, and for babysitting even when they didn't feel like it.

...to my sister, Mindy, for all the phone calls and fashion advice. (By the way, what should I wear if I get on *Oprah*?)

...to my *Simple* pals—Stacy, for believing in me; Angie, for waving the ScrapHappy flag; Jennafer, for trusting; Megan, for keeping everything on track; and Cathy, for making it all look good.

...to my readers, students, and scrapping friends, for sharing a bit of yourself with me.

{ CONTENTS }

ONE

Introduction: A Need-to-Know Basis

The first thing you should know about me is that I'm one of you. I take more pictures of my kids than I know what to do with, I hide bags from the scrapbook store under the dirty diapers in the garbage can so my husband won't find them, and I could wallpaper my house—and several other people's houses—with my stash of Bazzill cardstock. In a word, I'm a scrapbooker.

I started scrapping, as many of us do, when my first child was born in 1997. I attended one of those home-based consultant demos, and I dropped $100 on my own "personal cutting system," even though at that point in time I didn't know an eyelet from a hole in the ground. After diligently creating a few layouts (that in retrospect could easily qualify for the "before" layout in any makeover article), I stuffed it all in a drawer and forgot about it—almost.

Every so often, I'd flip through a roll of recently developed prints and stick them in a Buster Brown shoebox. A twinge of guilt would shoot through me as I saw them there, wrapped in their little white paper shrouds. "I should *do* something with these!" I'd say to myself. But then I'd have to go put in another Barney video or fix another batch of macaroni and cheese, or do something really self-indulgent like take a shower or brush my teeth. Scrapbooking just didn't fit in my busy new-mom life—I thought—and I'd push the idea over to the little corner of my brain earmarked "Someday."

Little did I know how soon "Someday" would come, and how much it would change my life. Today, more than a decade after my first date with scrapbooking, my life basically revolves around it (*and* my endless search for cute, mom-friendly shoes, but that's another story). Now, when I'm not actually creating layouts, I'm usually involved in some sort of peripheral scrapbooking activity—reading about it, writing articles about it for *Simple Scrapbooks* magazine, talking about it, blogging about it, teaching classes about it, looking at other people's scrapbook layouts, shopping for scrapbook supplies, or organizing my stash of stuff. I suppose it's sort of like being obsessed with golf—but a lot cheaper. At least, most of the time.

Call it a hobby, a passion, an addiction, or an obsession—the result is the same: I spend a lot more time and money on this activity than I ever thought possible. But I try not to question my motives too much. After all, there are many things in life that defy logic (like slip-on sneakers with laces, the popularity of thong underwear, and Britney Spears). So those close to me will just have to accept this little personality quirk of mine. I make no attempt to explain it, other than to say, "I'm a scrapbooker, and I'm proud." Now, about those bags hidden in the trash can...

TWO

Call Me a Collector

"Y ou have an illness," my husband said the other day when he walked into my craft closet.

I raised my head from the layout I was working on and looked around. "What are you talking about?" I asked.

"Just look," he said, gesturing to the piles surrounding me. "What are you holding onto all this old junk for?"

"What, these?" I asked, taking in the stacks to my left and right—and, I admit, above and below me. "These aren't junk. These are—these are magazines, my dear sir! This is the very stuff of which dreams are made! This is ART! Look, look at this!" I cried, waving a copy of *Scrapbook Answers* circa 2005 under his nose. "You can't buy this anymore! This is a collector's item! This would go for twenty bucks on eBay!"

He snorted. "Well, whatever they are, they're getting in the way of closing the closet door. And they're all over the bathroom floor."

I admit it. I do have a thing for scrapbook magazines and idea books. How could I possibly resist 100-odd pages of the latest and greatest in products and designs, delivered right to my doorstep? As a result, I've had as many as six monthly subscriptions going at any one time. Multiply that by a decade of scrapping, the purchase of an idea book or two each month, and you have...well, you have a lot of magazines.

I took a little tour around the house. Scrapbook magazines piled on my bedside table. Scrapbook magazines spilling out of the basket in the bathroom. Scrapbook magazines strewn across the floor in my office, tucked into my purse, stuck in the back seat pocket in the car, and arranged by season on the shelf in my craft closet. The house looked like it had been decorated in early *Creating Keepsakes*. Maybe my husband was right. Maybe I did have a few too many periodicals.

But where to start? I couldn't just toss the old issues. Some of them were classics—like the first issue of *Creating Keepsakes* where Heidi Swapp's byline appeared. Or, of course, a complete 7-year set of *Simple Scrapbooks* magazine (I plan to get these bound in leather someday). These weren't just magazines; they were *memories*!

Granted, there was a lot of material that I didn't need—old-style layouts that I'd never want to replicate, articles on Photoshop version 1.0, pages of ads for products now defunct. If I could just filter out that stuff, I could get my magazine stash down to a manageable level.

Once I had a plan, the solution was easy. I bought a dozen three-ring binders and few thousand sheet protectors, and settled myself on the couch for some serious selecting and sorting.

Eventually, I had a good-sized stack of images and articles to file by category—technique, color, articles, layouts. The articles were easy—I slipped them into page protectors and snapped them into the appropriate binder. The layouts were harder. They would require some thought.

"There, that's much better," I said, admiring my handiwork one evening.

"What are you *doing*?" my husband asked,

looking over my shoulder.

"I'm cleaning up, like you told me to," I replied, surprised. "What does it look like?"

"It looks like you're scrapbooking your old scrapbook magazines," he said.

I looked down at the table in front of me. I had discovered that I couldn't just paste an eclectic Elsie Flannigan next to a clean and simple Cathy Zielske, no more than I could create a single scrapbook layout with photos from Halloween and my parents' wedding day. I also had found that just sticking the cutout image on a page wasn't enough; occasionally, a little piece of ribbon or a button or two really set the design off. Was that weird?

"Are you *crazy*? Don't you have enough pictures to scrapbook, without wasting your time embellishing magazine articles?" he demanded.

I stopped for a minute. He had a point. I had likely crossed some line into scrapbook insanity that would not be easy to return from. And yet...my husband had properly used the word "embellish."

I must be doing something right.

THREE

Making Time

A common struggle in the scrapbooking arena is how to find time to actually sit down and get some good work done, with all the other demands in our frantic lives. We seem to be so busy living that we don't have time to document that life. Funny how that works, eh?

Time management experts recommend taking advantage of "dead" space, those unoccupied snippets of your day that are wasted on time-sucking tasks. These "experts" obviously haven't seen my schedule, as the only "dead" time available is the 30 seconds of reflection I have while I'm stopped at the red light at the corner of our street. In fact, I don't know of any female who has "spare" time. A woman's every waking moment is filled with tasks related to kids, jobs, spouses, or housework—not to mention the personal hygiene requirements that we need to fit in.

It seems that the average productivity expert is out of touch with the needs of the modern scrapbooking female. As a result, I have created this little list of strategies to fit more scrapbooking time into your daily allotment of 24 hours:

1. Break it up. Did you actually think your family would willingly let you out of their sight for hours on end? After all, you are the household's heart and soul—especially when you want some time to yourself. So drop your unrealistic expectations of long afternoons of uninterrupted playtime and get real. A stretch of 10 or 15 minutes is about all you can hope for, so use that time wisely by sketching layout ideas, choosing products for your next masterpiece, placing finishing touches on an almost-done design, or ordering photo prints. Sure, you aren't going to complete gift albums for both sets of grandparents in one sitting, but let's face it: your creativity wouldn't last that long anyway.

2. Lie. I know, I know, honesty is the best policy and all. But desperate times call for desperate measures. Do you really think your kids will be irreparably damaged because you told them "Mommy has a headache" before disappearing into your bedroom to crop for 30 minutes? Remember, husbands have been stretching the truth for generations (what do you think they're *really* doing behind the locked bathroom door for an hour at a time?) Which is worse—losing it completely and eating your way through the Häagen-Dazs in your freezer, or telling your kids a little fib and maintaining your sanity? You be the judge.

3. Contract a debilitating disease. Sure, it *sounds* a bit extreme, but just think! Hours of bed rest, no chores, and—if you manage to become hospitalized—catered meals, an adjustable bed, and a cute little tray that's the perfect size for 8 x 8 pages! Of course, there are drawbacks to this strategy, namely, possible death and disfigurement, so choose your illness wisely. Good: viral meningitis, strep, and sprained ankles. Bad: ebola, broken wrists, and pregnancy (yes, getting knocked up may sound good at the time, but at the end of nine months you'll be left with *more* on your plate, not less).

4. Pull a Houdini. No matter how small your house is, there have to be little hidey-holes where you can sequester yourself for a few minutes of free time. Good spots to try: in the bathtub (lock the bathroom door and turn the sink faucet on to further the deception, but try to stay dry), under the bed, and in the car. (Note: if you keep the motor running, make sure to leave the garage door open, lest you asphyxiate yourself inadvertently.) You'll have to get creative to actually accomplish anything in these tight spots, so forget the guillotine trimmers and Cricut die-cutting machines—instead think mini-albums and tags.

5. Use the trump card. In our house, everyone's in my face 24/7—that is, until I need them to finish their homework or help me with chores. Make this work for you: convert your laundry room into a joint utility/scrap space. Pull out the detergent, make a round through the rooms with the laundry basket, and announce loudly that you'd like to spend Saturday morning "working on the house." Watch the rest of the family scatter to parts unknown. Retire to your "laundry room" for an hour or two of undisturbed scrapbooking. Breathe deeply. Smile.

{ FOUR }

True Confessions

For the most part, I'm a good person. I recycle my cans, bottles, and paper. I pick up trash at the baseball field. I wave people into my lane on the highway, and I'm the first to volunteer for Sunday School duty when the church is shorthanded.

But somehow—I'm hesitant to say this, but I owe you nothing short of the complete truth—scrapbooking brings out the worst in me.

More than once, I've used multiple craft-store coupons in a single day, swooping in, snatching up an idea book, slapping down my 40 percent off coupon, and dashing out the door, only to return a few minutes later wearing a jacket, sunglasses, and a ball cap. I can't be certain, but I don't think the cashiers have noticed that the woman with a penchant for the latest Ali Edwards book is the same one who buys Glue Dots by the gross.

I've also enlisted my children in my efforts to save a few bucks. I shove hastily cropped coupons and $20 bills into their chubby little hands, and push them up to the cash register in front of me. So what if they can barely see over the counter? I'm prepared to swear on a stack of *Simple Scrapbooks* magazines that the Fiskars punches they're purchasing are for their personal use.

Those craft-store coupons are like crack to a craft addict like me. I've tried to convince my husband that we need to subscribe to the newspaper, just so I'll be sure to have at least one legitimate copy of the Sunday inserts. But he objects on moral grounds, assuming that he'd be enabling my substance abuse issues.

Subscription or not, I'll go to great lengths to get my hands on multiple copies of the Sunday paper. My favorite technique is to go through the newspaper rack at Starbucks, raiding the advertisement supplements in search of a bright yellow-and-red coupon. I've noticed a few raised eyebrows, but so far no one has stopped me to ask why I'm confiscating all the craft-store inserts from the *San Jose Mercury News*. Of course, they know me at my Starbucks, so they probably don't need to ask.

The bottom of the barrel, though, came the night I considered going dumpster diving in search of extra craft-store coupons. It was last year, just after a big tradeshow, and all sorts of new goodies were beginning to hit the shelves. Being way too cheap to pay full retail price, I made my usual pass by Starbucks on Sunday afternoon and was distraught to discover that the employees had already emptied the newspaper rack into the large dumpster in the parking lot.

I briefly thought of hopping in the 10' x 10' front-loader, but as tenuous as my reputation already is, I couldn't afford to inflict any more damage on my public image. So I came up with the bright idea of digging through the neighbors' recycling bins. Problem: the bins wouldn't be curbside until garbage pick-up day, which was four days away, and I had an urge to shop IMMEDIATELY.

So I did what any self-respecting scrapbooker-on-a-budget would do. I waited until after dark and drove to my *parents'* street to pillage the neighborhood recycling bins. For days afterward, I kept expecting a knock on my door and a visit from the boys in blue, but so far I've escaped capture

Yeah, scrapbooking has at times appealed to my baser instincts—the ones that compel me to hoard alpha stickers and 7gypsies charms. But I still feel like I have at least a modicum of control over the situation. After all, I could have forced my *children* to go through the neighbors' recycling bins...hey, that's not a bad idea! I could drive them around town, letting them out to collect newspapers door-to-door. And if anyone asks them what they're doing, I'll tell my kids to say they're gathering recyclables to help the less fortunate. It wouldn't be *that* far from the truth.

{ FIVE }

A Friend in Need...

Forget about the 12-inch portable paper trimmer. Forget about the silent eyelet setter. Forget about the Xyron sticker maker, the personal die cut machine, and the acid-free photo pen. While all these are grand inventions in their own right, the single biggest innovation to ever hit the scrapbooking world is: the Internet.

To the non-scrapper, "Internet" and "scrapbooking" may not seem to go hand-in-hand. But anyone who's ever picked up a tape runner knows that she could not scrap without her high-speed Internet hookups—both literal and figurative.

Just think about it. Before the Internet, how did people know where to find the lowest price on American Crafts albums? How did people keep up to date on the latest scrap celebrity happenings? How did people compare ideas for enlivening Little League layouts, debate the best way to adhere twill to the page, or share the angst of trying to get noticed by the editors of *Scrappin' Digest*?

And most of all, how did scrapbookers find each other?

Scrapbooking can be a lonely hobby. Husbands usually don't understand the obsession with all things lignin-free, and even the most dedicated memory keepers are often cursed with friends and family members who don't know a binder ring from a jump ring—and don't *want* to know.

Some of us are lucky enough to live within close proximity to a well-stocked scrapbook store, where we can meet like-minded souls. But for many of our sister scrappers, it's easier to find a restaurant with Fresca on tap than it is to find a retail establishment that sells single sheets of Foof-a-la. Thus, if it weren't for the Internet—and its scrapper-specific bulletin boards, online communities, and Yahoo groups—a good portion of our ilk would live lives of quiet desperation, having no one with whom to share the trials and tribulations of hand-cutting titles and getting chipboard letters to stick on a page.

I think there are a couple of reasons why online scrapbooking communities are so popular. First, despite the fact that we journal on our pages because we want to share our stories, scrapbooking can be a very private hobby. The longer you do it, the deeper and more personal your pages become. And if you're going to journal about your stint as an exotic dancer, or your ambivalence about having breast augmentation surgery, you'll probably feel more comfortable sharing those stories online with a virtual (no pun intended) stranger, than with the gal you're sitting next to at Free Crop Night—a gal you just might run into at church or at the next PTA meeting.

Second, scrapbookers are round-the-clock crafters. Yes, our free time may occasionally coincide with Archiver's business hours, but more likely than not, we're going to be needing that poem about the dead goldfish at 2 AM instead of 2 PM. And at any time, day or night, we can boot up the computer, safe in the knowledge that someone, somewhere—Australia? Madrid? Spokane?—will appreciate our creative use of deckle-edged scissors on our latest layout.

Any scrapper worth her glitter would argue that the friends she's made online are just as supportive and just as important as those who live next door or across town. Whether we loan them our copy of *Digital Designs for Scrapbooking* in person or send it via UPS doesn't matter; the bond between two scrapbookers is stronger than any double-sided tape.

Non-scrapbookers might not get this. "How can you feel so deeply about and spend so much time with people you've never met *in real life*?" they ask. Little do they know that the hours we spend online are just as real—if not more so—than the hours we spend with our "real" friends and family.

It's okay if they don't get it, though. They probably don't understand the need for seven different kinds of adhesive, either.

{ SIX }

Scrapper's Brain

Never again, I told myself. After last year's Christmas-card debacle, which involved trying to stamp with pigment ink on vellum (note: it doesn't work) and spending 15 minutes and $2 per card (amounting to 37 hours and $300 total), I swore never to make my own Christmas cards again.

That resolution lasted all of 11 months.

I promised myself that I'd handle the whole thing differently this year. No vellum. No hand-tied ribbons. No hand-cut cardstock. Yes, I would make my own cards (as a self-respecting scrapbooker, how could I not?). But I'd cut my recipient list to 75 instead of 150. And I'd do a *simple* card. A photo. A sticker. A square of cardstock. And that would be it.

Ha.

Sure, it started out that way. I got a box of pre-fab cards from Die Cuts With a View for the bargain price of $7, and I decided I'd have my resident artist (my 6-year-old daughter) draw a picture for the front. I would then color-copy the artwork, adhere it to the front of the card, stamp a greeting, and *voila!* I'd be done.

Everything proceeded smoothly...for about 5 minutes. Not to point fingers or anything, but the resident artist did *not* follow instructions. She submitted not one but two separate drawings, and they were so cute that there was no way I could use only one.

And then I got a bad case of Scrapper's Brain. You know how it goes. *"Wouldn't this look cute if I mounted it on some holiday-themed patterned paper?"* your Scrapper's Brain asks, and you agree. And so you buy a few (hundred) sheets of Christmas paper. *"Wouldn't this look even cuter if I matted it on white cardstock to make it stand out more?"* your Scrapper's Brain continues. And so you start cutting and matting. *"But wait,"* your Scrapper's Brain interrupts. *"Just think how great it would look if you distressed the edges of the white cardstock with some red paint!"* And distress you do. After all, you are no longer in control. Your

Scrapper's Brain has taken over.

"That wasn't so bad," you say finally, with a sigh. *"No problem."*

But your Scrapper's Brain isn't finished with you yet.

Your Scrapper's Brain wants you to add the tiny metal Making Memories Christmas bulb embellishments you bought last year on clearance.

Your Scrapper's Brain wants you to thread ⅛" ribbon through each of these bulbs before you glue them on.

Your Scrapper's Brain also wants you to add 20 more people to your Christmas card list, which means returning to the craft store to buy another box of DCWV cards.

And to top it all off, your Scrapper's Brain also wants you to write a cheery, clever Christmas missive (oh, wait, that wasn't your Scrapper's Brain, that was your Writer's Brain. I sometimes get them confused).

But when it comes time to hand-address all the cards and design the festive return address labels, is your Scrapper's Brain there to help? Nooo. And where is your Scrapper's Brain while you're standing in line for 37 minutes at the post office, only to be left with two choices of stamps— Domestic Violence or Superheroes—neither of which seemed particularly holiday-ish? Nowhere to be found.

Your Scrapper's Brain has disappeared...until next year.

{ SEVEN }

A Room of One's Own

I've got a shameful secret. It involves spending long hours cruising the Web, looking at enticing photos that cause my heart to race and my breath to quicken. Fortunately, this habit doesn't require a valid credit card number or a parental warning on the computer screen. All the same, it's a bit embarrassing. But, we're friends, right? So here it is: I'm addicted to other people's scrap rooms.

The level of my dedication is nothing short of scary. I can spend hours breathlessly clicking through link after link, drooling while I bookmark sites and save particularly provocative photos to my hard drive. Forget about Internet romances; I'm having an emotional affair with a Pottery Barn desk-and-bookshelf combo I saw online last week.

The idea that some scrapbookers have perfectly organized workspaces—complete with matching furniture and coordinated storage containers—is as far from my reality as my waistline is from Nicole Richie's. It's astonishing to me that people have scrap rooms large enough to host a dozen friends and their Cropper Hoppers, with room left over for a few full-spectrum floor lamps.

Okay, so I'm jealous. I live in Northern California, land of the silicon computer chip and the million-dollar "starter" home. Real estate is at a premium, and the price tag on my ideal scrapping space would have as many zeroes as a college tuition bill. And while I'd gladly trade my kids' future for a room of my own, my husband has me on a tight leash.

As a result, my scrap room is more of a "scrap broom," as in "broom closet." Exactly how diminutive is my room? Let me put it this way—the previous occupant of our home used this space for handbag storage. And the only way I could host a friend for a crop night would be to suspend us both from the ceiling in hammocks, Gilligan-and-the-Skipper style. Not only would that be a tad bit uncomfortable, it would also make it really hard to set an eyelet without cracking someone's coconut.

I'm not complaining, though. I know some women who are forced to house all of their scrapping paraphernalia inside a single armoire. Now, an armoire may *sound* fancy, but it's really just a French word meaning: "place to shove all your junk to keep it out of sight." The idea of having to pull everything out and put it back again each time I want to scrap is enough to keep me using magnetic photo albums for the rest of my natural-born life.

Maybe someday I'll have that dream room, the one with the cute white furniture and 12 x 12 file drawers. In the meantime, I'll stick to my voyeuristic tendencies, envying other women's floor space and wondering how they keep their desktops so clean. Seriously, how can you scrap without generating the least bit of clutter? You know, I bet they stash away those itty-bitty paper slivers, hole-punch chads, and unsorted products just long enough to take a nice picture—kind of like how I suck in my stomach and lift my head for the camera, and then let my chin rejoin my neck after the flash.

Honestly, you never really get a good look at the rest of the house in these photos, do you? All you ever see is the "scrap room." For all we know, they have all seven of their children piled into one bedroom, clothes bulging from the closets, the older kids sleeping under the beds, while the little ones doze in the dresser drawers.

Actually, that's not a bad idea. My three kids don't need all that space—after all, the only thing they do in their rooms is sleep. And now that I think about it, why do we need a living room *and* a family room? If we just consolidated a little, I'd have more scrapping room than I'd know what to do with. My husband won't mind if I use his half of the closet, either. If he needs someplace to put his clothes, I can always get him an armoire.

{ EIGHT }

A Bit of
Scrapbook Magic

As a child, I listened to fairy tales with a hearty dose of skepticism and outright disbelief. I mean, c'mon! What girl in her right mind would ask her fairy godmother for a pair of glass slippers instead of a Lexus or a good chunk of Intel stock? Magic, to me, seemed to be one more way for parents to convince their kids to do what they were told. Example: "If you are a good little girl, Santa will bring you whatever you want." Yeah, right—that trick stopped working the year I demanded a cocker spaniel puppy in place of my baby sister, and Old Saint Nick failed to deliver.

When I became a scrapbooker, however, I discovered that certain experiences lay well beyond my powers of rationalization. Strange happenings were afoot, and I was at a loss to justify them. Thus, I present, for your reading pleasure, a rundown of "magical" events that I've borne witness to over the past decade:

1. ESP. My kids have a sixth sense when it comes to knowing when Mom has the camera in her hand. The three of them can be snuggling on the couch, cute as can be, engaged in a rare moment of sibling adoration. All I have to do is to pull out my Kodak and suddenly they're monsters. The little one will immediately stick her finger up her brother's nose, the middle one will smack her sister on the head and make her cry, and the oldest will enter the "no-smile zone," where no amount of coaxing can get him to crack a grin. I can yell, plead, and bribe, but the only real way to get them to revert to their previous cuteness is to put the camera away.

2. Mind-Reading. I can personally attest to the existence of telepathy. I know without a doubt what my husband is thinking when I enter the house clutching a bag from the scrapbook store. And he can read my mind as well. Our telepathic abilities are so strong that we can have complete conversations without opening our mouths. If you could see us, you'd detect some raised eyebrows and expressive shrugs, but the real dialog is taking place just beneath the surface. Let's listen in on one of these mental exchanges:

John's Brain: "You went to the scrapbook store again? Don't you have enough stuff already?"

My Brain: "I ran out of adhesive."

J.B.: "Isn't adhesive the sticky stuff? Why is that bag full of patterned paper?"

M.B.: "It's just a few sheets. The new American Crafts came in. I can always use more paper."

J.B.: "More paper? You mean the five reams you have upstairs aren't enough?"

M.B.: "That's OLD paper. I needed the NEW stuff."

J.B.: "It all looks the same to me."

M.B.: "All the football games you watch look the same to me, too, but you don't see me giving you a hard time about it."

J.B.: "Whatever."

M.B.: "Exactly."

3. Invisibility/Time Travel. Things disappear around my craft area with alarming regularity. To date, I have sacrificed two corner rounders, three pairs of scissors, and an entire bag of purchases from a very cool scrapbook store in Los Angeles.

No, I did not misplace these items; my scrap room is not big enough to actually *lose* anything. The only possible explanations are that they've become invisible, or that they've been sucked into some rip in the space-time continuum. I, for one, wouldn't be surprised if some cavewoman in prehistoric Asia is now looking with bafflement at a sheet of Foof-a-la stickers that suddenly appeared on her bearskin rug.

4. Precognition. Want to see me predict the future? Here it is: I predict that tonight after dinner, none of my children will want anything to do with me. That is, until I sit down at my scrapbook table and try to get some time to myself. Then, suddenly, I will become the most popular person in the house. Top that, Nostradamus.

So there you have it. I admit it. Magic does exist, and it's alive and well in my scrapbook room. Now, if only my fairy godmother would appear. She can, however, forget the glass slippers, the ball gown, and even the Lexus. If she's interested in making my wildest fantasies come true, I could really use a top-of-the-line wide-format printer.

NINE

Invincible

The best thing about scrapbooking is that it makes you feel like you can do anything. The worst thing about scrapbooking? It makes you feel like you can do anything.

Let me explain. There's something about becoming competent in one area of your life that makes you feel like you can translate that success elsewhere. Like when you finally learn how to operate your KitchenAid mixer, you suddenly think you're prepared to host a six-course Thanksgiving dinner for the whole clan, including creating Martha Stewart-esque handcrafted centerpieces from organic fruits and vegetables. Or once you get your black belt in karate, you feel you're instantly capable of chatting with the chef at the local sushi bar—in Japanese. Or, if you're like me, once you get the hang of this scrapbooking thing, you realize you've been automatically imbued with 50 extra IQ points, the skills to master any and all power tools, and the ability to undertake any home improvement project with style and grace.

Little do you know, you're completely delusional.

The delusions kind of sneak up on you. At first, they're no big deal. Instead of calling the hubby to take the lid off the pickle jar, you decide to get out your Making Memories eyelet-setting hammer and smack the darned thing into submission yourself. No problem.

But your feelings of competency spread. You find yourself wondering why you'd pay someone else—someone with far less design sense, artistic ability, and experience with adhesive than you—to decorate your daughter's birthday cake. After all, you're a scrapbooker! Butter-cream frosting and sprinkles? That's nothing compared to working with cranky rhinestones and alphabet stickers the size of gnats!

And from there, it makes total sense that you would create your own bulletin boards for the kids' rooms instead of just using boring, ready-made ones. A little patterned paper and a bit of acrylic paint does work up nicely on corkboard from the craft store, no arguing with that.

Then, you notice that your family-room wall could use a little sprucing up. Your pre-scrapbooking approach would be to comb through home décor magazines in search of walls to emulate. You would then sort and piece together your magazine clippings, deconstructing and reconstructing, until you came up with a combination of photo frames, floral arrangements, sconces, and a paint color that looked pretty good. Then you'd ask your significant other to take a look and make suggestions. You'd argue with him about his ideas, throw the whole thing out, and call the interior designer who did your best friend's neighbor's kitchen.

Not so for the scrapper! After all, a family-room wall is really just a big scrapbook page, right? And weren't you the one who successfully arranged 27 photos from your family reunion into an eye-catching, two-page spread—despite the fact that everyone was wearing clashing colors and your uncle Sid had that awful skin rash? A family-room wall? Pshaw! No so-called "experts" needed here!

And all in all, the family-room wall doesn't turn

out too bad. Yeah, that particular shade of yellow might look a little less psychedelic on a sheet of 12 x 12 Bazzill cardstock. And the addition of rub-ons in the corners of the windows would have been okay if you hadn't gone the extra step and adhered dozens of die-cut flowers down the panes.

And can you really blame your husband for getting upset when you moved the flat screen HDTV from the center of the wall to the lower left corner, behind the door, because it provided better design balance? And maybe drilling holes in a random pattern and filling them with colored grout wasn't one of your better ideas. I know, they kind of looks like eyelets, and I understand that you didn't do any real structural damage...and I totally get that "the rule of threes" demanded that you cut two more openings in the wall to create a "visual triangle" that includes the door to the hallway.

But you may be getting just a tiny bit beyond your skills. Maybe—just maybe—you should rein yourself in. Maybe you should take a hint when your husband hides the power tools from you.

Then again...maybe not.

{ TEN }

ScrapCouture: The Height of Fashion

After I dragged my fashionable (yet impractical) bell sleeve across a freshly laid path of glitter glue for the umpteenth time, I had to ask, why is it that there are no scrapbook-friendly clothes?

At first, that seems like a silly question. Why on earth would scrapbookers need hobby-specific garb? But humor me while we explore the idea a little further. We've all heard that scrapbooking is more popular than golf. And golfers wear those funny little shoes and silly pants, right? Bowlers have bowling shoes. Fishermen have floppy hats, waders, and ugly vests. Even *polo players* have their own wardrobe, which has been adopted by the preppy crowd. When is the last time you met an actual, pony-riding, Ralph Lauren-wearing, mallet-wielding enthusiast?

Is it really so crazy to think that fashion designers might see us—23 million strong, after all—as a viable market segment? Yes, we're starting to see some cute and kitschy scrapbook-related t-shirts (my favorite: "It's all fun and games until someone loses an eyelet"). But slogan t-shirts aren't enough. I truly believe that it's only a matter of time before we see entire racks in the "Women's Active" section of Nordstrom devoted to what I call "ScrapCouture." And to help the fashion moguls get it right the first time, here are a few things for Donatella, Vera, and Tommy to consider:

1. Color. If there's one fashion innovation that would make my life easier, it would be a selection of shirts carefully color-coordinated to match my favorite stamp pads, paints, and pens. How often have I irreparably stained my sleeve—and smeared my page—by unintentionally besmirching a recent paint job? A simple, cotton-blend, v-necked tee in Ranger's Adirondack Sunset Orange, Eggplant, and Bright Raspberry would solve a lot of problems. Sure, the pages would still smear, but there'd be no visible evidence left on me.

2. Form. I know that wide, long sleeves are in

fashion. I know that designers are moving toward richer, more lavish materials. But these trends just don't fit the scrapper's life. I need wash-and-wear, people! I need close-fitting and snug, but not *too* snug. I need comfort and convenience, not runway-ready. The last thing I want to do when I'm creating is to be thinking about a too-tight waistband or an itchy lace panel. Let's face it—if I could scrap in a full-length bodysuit, I would. But since that's out for aesthetic reasons, let's see if we can develop a suitable substitute: a washable, short-sleeved bathrobe, perhaps, or an A-line, empire-waisted, three-quarter-sleeved dress would be nice.

   3. Function. As a multi-tasking mom, the more functions a single garment can perform for me, the better. I want an outfit that will take me from scrap room to classroom to boardroom, and if it looks a little hip and trendy, all the better. How about a full-length apron that, with just a few strategic ties and drapes, turns into a kimono-style jacket? Or a wrap skirt that can double as a drop cloth if you decide to spray paint your latest album creation, and you need to cover your desk and office chair in a hurry? I'd even settle for a reversible t-shirt that I could whip off and turn inside-out, concealing any tell-tale glue smears, when the clock strikes 2:30 and I'm steaming out the door to pick up the kids from school. (I do this now, but the other moms tend to give me a wide berth when they see me with my clothes on inside-out and that wild, "been scrappin' all day" look in my eyes).

With the fashion industry's constant desire to introduce the new, the different, the innovative, it seems like ScrapCouture is an inevitable part of the future. In the meantime, though, I'm going to keep wearing my ink-stained jeans and glue-encrusted t-shirts. And maybe if I slap a "Pearl Jam" bumper sticker on my car and start carrying a copy of Kurt Cobain's diaries, people will just consider me retro-grunge, rather than hopelessly sloppy. Hey, it's worth a shot.

ELEVEN

Other People's Photos

I am a brave woman. I dispose of spiders without batting an eye, either picking them up by their furry little legs and depositing them outside, or squishing them into oblivion and flushing the evidence. I can handle blood, wiggly baby teeth, and the scariest of diapers without a second thought. But despite my fortitude in many areas of everyday life, there's one situation I avoid at all costs. And my vast years of experience compel me to pass some words of warning on to you:

If someone asks you to scrap their pictures for them, *just say no!*

It doesn't matter how innocent it seems: a simple baby album, a Christmas page or two, or—horrors upon horrors!—a wedding album. Don't do it!

You may think that, as an experienced scrapbooker with years under your belt, creating a little album for a friend, neighbor, or relation would be a piece of cake. You've got the talent, not to mention the supplies, so isn't it stingy to keep it all to yourself?

Believe me when I tell you that, should you agree to create "a little something" for someone else, you may very well be heading straight down the path to the Underworld. And the worst part is, the more you care about that other person, the more the universe suggests—no, *demands*—that you refuse.

I'm not talking about an end-of-the-year scrapbook for your daughter's first-grade teacher, or a mini-album for your son's soccer coach. Even blank albums to be handed over to a newly minted mom and dad are perfectly acceptable.

What I'm warning you against is taking a nice, little box full of other people's photos (their very memories, in other words) and attempting to scrapbook them.

Sure, it can be done, but at what cost? How many hours are you willing to sacrifice, flipping through the contents of that box, looking at photo after photo, trying to figure out if it's really critical that you include that particular shot of Aunt Maude? Yes, it's the only surviving photo of her, but should you overlook the irrefutable proof that she's just imbibed a tad too much sherry? How much stress are you going to put on yourself, attempting to interpret the handwriting of some long-dead amateur historian? Does the notation really say "Joseph and Paul, in drag," or is it "Josie and Paula, with flag?" And does the caption on this snapshot say "Dougie looking cute," or "Donald looking fat?" You'd need a degree in hieroglyphics to know for sure.

Heritage photos are bad news, because chances are, they're irreplaceable. One little slip of the Fiskars snips and you may easily destroy the only pictorial evidence that your friend's ancestors really were aboard the very first ship to land at Ellis Island, or exactly which side they fought for in the Civil War. Get a little sloppy with the tape runner, and suddenly that priceless photo from 1818 isn't so priceless anymore.

But no matter how tough it is to work with heritage photos, the worst of all are the wedding pictures. The truth is, wedding portraits are numbered among every woman's most precious possessions. It was the one day of her life that she truly felt like a princess, and by messing around with the pictures from that day—even at her request—you are toying with her memories. You'd think there was no such thing as duplicates, the way most brides act about their photos. (And every woman, no matter how long it's been since her wedding day, is still a bride.) You'd be better off remodeling another woman's kitchen, or trying to give her baby his first haircut, than messing with her bridal photos.

So, you may be wondering, what do you do when your cousin or your husband's boss's daughter asks you to create a little album from her treasured stash of pictures? First, take a deep breath. Second, smile sweetly. Then say, "You know, no one would do a better job preserving *your* memories than you. And I'd be glad to help you get started."

There. Not only have you saved yourself hours of misery and strife, you've also converted a potential scrapbooker.

Score one for the good guys.

TWELVE

Mommy Dearest

On my scrapping desk I've got a glass jar full of change. Every day I add a few coins to my collection. No, it's not a fund to purchase the new Cricut personal die cutting system, and I'm not saving up to attend CKU-Provo next year (although maybe *some* of the money could be used for that!). Instead, this fund is for my kids. Well, not for them, exactly—it's for their future therapy.

Let's face it: a life as the child of a scrapbooker is not an easy one. I fully expect someday in the not-too-distant future to get a call from a psychiatrist, asking me to explain the parental actions that smashed my child's ego and trod upon his id (do people still talk about ids?).

And the worst part is, the doc will be right. I'm guilty.

I'm guilty of forcing my kids to pose for hours, or sometimes *days*, on end, with the sun burning into their corneas, as I click away in search of "the perfect shot." I'm guilty of dressing all three of them in matching outfits and parading them through hotel lobbies, encouraging them to "act natural," all in the name of Christmas card photos. I'm guilty of spending the last day of our vacation in Hawaii driving hundreds of miles in search of the island's only scrapbook store. And I'm guilty of missing more than one bedtime story by responding to "just a couple more" blog comments on my upstairs computer.

Yup. I've done them all.

But before I get nominated for the Joan Crawford Mother of the Year award, let's review what I *didn't* do (but sure could have):

I *didn't* make all three of them share the same room so I could turn the biggest bedroom in the house into my "scrap studio." Instead, I suffer with a small 5' x 7' windowless closet, while they get huge, airy rooms that they barely use except to sleep.

I *didn't* sell my son's prized Yu-Gi-Oh cards on eBay so I could buy the complete line of Prima flowers. Instead, I make do with a measly bottle or two and give those cards dirty looks every time

I see them lying tossed aside on the family-room floor or crumpled under the seat of the car.

I *didn't* make my daughter have a Care Bears birthday party so I could use those adorable papers and embellishments I saw at the local scrapbook store. Instead, I let her choose her own theme (alien cowgirl???), even though I had a devil of a time finding fluorescent green cowboy boot and hat stickers.

I *didn't* scream and banish my toddler to the basement the day I came into my scrapping closet and saw that she'd gotten "creative" with my entire stock of glitter, sequins, and Aleene's Jewel-It. Instead, I chuckled indulgently, took a few photos for posterity, then got out the DustBuster.

I *didn't* miss the first day of school so I could attend that scrap-and-cruise getaway to Baja. Instead, I stood there in line with the other moms as my kids ignored me completely and ran off to their classrooms without a backwards glance, leaving me with 24 pictures of their backs.

I didn't do any of these things. But when that psychiatrist of the future calls me into his office to read me the riot act, I've got my defense all planned.

I'll stare down that accusatory finger and tell him the biggest thing I didn't do.

"I didn't miss a moment," I'll tell him. "For all my shortcomings and errors as a mother, I was there for all of it—the good, the bad, the in-between. And I captured it all, right here between the pages of these books." And then I'll present Exhibits A through Z, and I'll pile load upon load of scrapbooks onto his desk, burying him beneath my carefully preserved memories.

And then I'll hand him the jar of quarters, nickels, and pennies and hope it covers his fee.

{ THIRTEEN }

Look, Ma, No Hands!

Have you noticed that whole "extreme" trend that seems to be taking over our culture? *Everything* is extreme these days. I kind of understood the extreme sports thing, where people strap on some skis, jump out of a helicopter, and slalom down Mt. Everest. But I just saw an article about "extreme knitting." What's up with that? Does that mean you knit a pair of socks without a pattern? Or maybe it means you knit while jumping out of a helicopter on skis?

In any case, I figure if knitters can be extreme, scrapbookers can be, too. There's nothing like a little friendly rivalry between the crafts to get the competitive juices going. But unlike those yarn devotees, we will set certain guidelines. We will only deem our scrapbooking "extreme" if it can meet the following criteria:

1. **Emotional risk.** There has to be an element

of risk to what you're attempting. Soul-baring, heart-on-the-sleeve journaling that shares details of psychic trauma definitely counts. As does using permanent adhesive on your heritage photos instead of removable, or cutting into an original wedding photo without making a copy first. Extra points for scrapping recent photos of yourself clad in a bikini; double points for submitting the page for publication; and triple points if the page then appears in a nationally distributed magazine.

2. Danger. For an activity to truly qualify as "extreme," physical danger is a must. Yes, papercuts can be quite painful, but I doubt anyone would consider them "dangerous." And while the tools in the scrapbooker's arsenal (craft hammer and paper piercer, for starters) are far riskier than even the most extreme knitter's tools (two pointy sticks and ball of fuzz?), I still think we can do better. What about getting out an actual power drill instead of that cute, pink handheld doohickey by Fiskars? And who's up for hand-cutting their titles out of cardstock with a Bowie knife? Now we're talking "extreme."

3. Impossible odds. "Extreme," to me, also means stretching the limits of what is possible.

And who better to attempt the impossible than a scrapbooker? We're known for setting seemingly unachievable goals, like scrapbooking all 5,000 digital photos from our child's first five years of life. Or creating two matching "this is your life" albums for Grandma and Grandpa's golden wedding anniversary—by next Thursday. Impossible! Or is it?

4. General repugnance. We scrapbookers are also known for taking on projects no one else wants to do—projects that are so bad a normal person would rather remove her own tonsils with a pair of decorative scissors than attempt. We're like contestants on *The Fear Factor,* but instead of crunching down on raw squid entrails or letting tarantulas crawl all over our nether regions, we do other terrifying things. We agree to make individualized scrapbooks for each of the 60 children in kindergarten. We decide to coordinate the baseball coach's season-end gift scrapbook, which doesn't sound so bad until you realize you have to convince fifteen 9-year-old boys to stop punching each other long enough to pick up a pair of craft scissors and a glue stick.

5. Extreme conditions. You know what I mean

by "extreme conditions"—I mean trying to make 15 *Shrek* birthday party invitations the night before your youngest wants to pass them out at school, only to discover that you're completely out of green cardstock, your last adhesive runner just hit empty, and your paper cutter has gone missing. Also included in this category is scrapbooking on school vacations (i.e., when the children are actually in the house) or trying to craft while your spouse is in the same room, interrupting you every 5 minutes with inane questions like what you're making for dinner and where you keep the extra lightbulbs.

Maybe scrapbooking is not as dangerous as jumping over a pit of burning coals on a minibike, or abalone diving in the Maldives, let alone tackling Mt. Everest on a pair of skis. But still, I challenge any one of those "extreme athletes" to sit down with a stack of 4 x 6 prints and a pile of cardstock and see what happens to *their* cardiovascular system. I don't need a helicopter ride to send my heart racing; I'm struck with palpitations every time I step into a scrapbook store. But that might just be the intoxicating aroma of freshly printed patterned paper.

FOURTEEN

Scrapper's Purse

After suffering through several weeks with a sharp ache in my right shoulder, I finally decided it was time to head to the doctor for a diagnosis. Maybe I had tendonitis. Maybe signing those 200 Christmas cards had overstressed my rotator cuff.

I told my husband my thoughts, certain that my ailments would generate at least a little bit of sympathy (and possibly even get me out of laundry duty for a few days). John took one look at the huge, black patent-leather purse I had slung over my shoulder—my right shoulder—and said, "Could it be your purse?"

What a ridiculous thought. Of course it wasn't my purse. I laughed scornfully at my know-nothing husband and dropped my purse with a clunk on the floor, smashing my little toe. "Hmmm, maybe this bag is a bit on the heavy side," I thought as I hopped up and down in pain. (Note: thoughts edited to be suitable for publication.) What was in there anyway?

Here's what I found:

• The latest issues of *Simple Scrapbooks* and *Cards,* two magazines I never leave home without. You never know when you might get stuck in traffic or at the dentist's office and need some solid reading material or a few ideas for a "Welcome Baby!" card for your new nephew.

• An altered coupon storage book, complete with coupons for every craft, scrapbook, and fabric store within a 40-mile radius.

• A pack of pictures I just picked up from the developer, containing almost 50 different shots, plus doubles and 5 x 7 enlargements.

• A complete set of Zig pens in a range of colors and pen-tip sizes.

• A deck of playing cards, minus the ace of hearts, the three of spades, and both jokers, which I rescued (for a future creative project, of course) as my husband was attempting to toss it in the trash.

• A mini-journal for jotting down funny things my kids say, such as the moment the other day when my three-year-old told me to "just chill, Mom."

• A handheld digital voice recorder for capturing memories, thoughts, and ideas for future scrapbook layouts on the fly.

• An altered calendar, loaded up with buttons, ribbons, and other weighty embellishments.

• Half of a keychain, which I salvaged from the parking lot outside the karate studio last week, with the intention of prying it apart and using it on an upcoming mini-album for my father.

• Frequent buyer cards for the four scrapbook stores within an hour's drive of my house.

• Four empty treat bags (decorated with snowmen) from a party my daughter attended. She wanted to throw them out, but I had big plans for them.

• A wallet containing three lonely dollar bills, my driver's license, credit cards, and a stack of receipts from the craft store. (Hey, I'm a professional—this stuff is tax-deductible!)

• My iPod Shuffle, loaded with podcasts about crafting and creativity.

• A copy of the exercise-class schedule for the local gym (wishful thinking, I know).

• A rubber band-wrapped stash of memorabilia from a recent family vacation that hasn't quite made its way to my scrap desk, where it will ultimately be added as ephemera to the pages of the vacation album that I've yet to plan and complete.

• Five ballpoint pens.

• And last, but certainly not least, my Kodak point-and-shoot.

So, what was the big deal? I *needed* all that stuff. You never know when you may get caught in an elevator and have the urge to read/scrap/take pictures of something. I like to be prepared.

At the same time, though, I had to admit that the weight of the bag was, well, weighing me down. I looked around at the piles of equipment, mementos, and soon-to-be craft projects surrounding me. Maybe it was a little excessive. After all, I had my health to consider.

So, I tossed the exercise schedule into the recycling bin, transferred three of the pens to the kitchen counter, and loaded everything else back in my bag.

Hey, it could be worse, I reasoned. I could own a Canon Digital Rebel. Those things weigh at least 5 pounds—and that's without the extra lenses.

FIFTEEN

Gotta Hand it to Ya

I was leafing through a paper-crafting magazine the other day (a common occurrence, as you might guess). I stopped to read an article on how to perform a particular technique—creating your own chandelier out of polymer clay, perhaps, or using your eyelet setting tools to hotwire a car—and I just had to laugh.

Like most women, I feel slightly inadequate when I compare myself to the standards of beauty set forth in the bevy of women's magazines I see in the grocery store checkout line. But I know that I am not (and never will be) Drew Barrymore, so I can usually put any thoughts of inferiority immediately to rest.

But for some reason, I'm hit much harder by the standards of beauty I see in the pages of my favorite scrapbooking magazines. In one particular periodical I was reading recently, page after page featured tightly cropped photographs of an armless set of hands, gracefully demonstrating each project, step by step. The hands were lovely—tan, but not too tan. Long, slender, unblemished fingers. Perfect French manicure tipping inch-long gel/acrylic nails. I sighed as I perused the issue, learning how to cut here, fold there, crease, and then score.

I sighed because I once had hands like that. But that was years ago, before I started scrapbooking.

So what's the deal here? Do Ali Edwards and Stacy Julian have "hand doubles" who stand in for them during photo shoots for their books and magazines? Do they hire someone with picture-perfect cuticles to pose from the wrist down and demonstrate their techniques? I'm wondering because I—and pretty much every other scrapbooker I know—have scrapper's hands.

You know what I'm talking about: nails that are so short they barely reach the tips of my fingers, decorated with not a speck of nail polish (unless some residual Ranger's Distress Ink in Worn Lipstick counts). Hangnails galore, a direct result of the frequent hand washing I endure in a futile attempt to get the adhesive and other goop off my fingers (not to mention the way solvent-based stamp pads can dry out the skin). A papercut across the right index finger. Small, brad-induced blood blisters—from trying to pry open the prongs of a brad, only to slip and feel a stabbing sensation on the sensitive skin beneath the nail bed. Calluses on the right thumb (from scissors) and the ring finger (from holding a pen).

But no matter how I may long for those French manicure days, they are gone. The polish was always chipping anyway, and the long, thick nails made it next to impossible to tie bows or pick up small embellishments. Plus, I've found that if I have a spare hour, I'd rather spend it creating something than sitting in a chair, getting my bi-weekly manicure and fill.

But you know what? I like scrapper's hands, despite their bumps and bruises. They look like hands that can do things—make 30 die-cut treat boxes for a little girl's Halloween party, for example, or write a letter to a son listing all the reasons the world is a better place because he was born.

Or, if so inclined, they could certainly make a chandelier from polymer clay. Or hotwire a car using eyelet setting tools.

SIXTEEN

All in the Family

The best thing in the world happened yesterday. Nope, I didn't win the *Creating Keepsakes'* Scrapbooker of the Year contest. I didn't get selected for the BasicGrey design team or receive an all-expenses-paid trip for two to the Scrappin' on Maui retreat. What happened was better: my sister spent the day scrapbooking with me.

Now, that may not sound very momentous. After all, according to the industry statistics, millions of people are scrapbooking at any given moment (and if they aren't scrapbooking, they're probably online looking at scrapbooking layouts).

The noteworthy thing about scrapbooking with my sister is that IT WAS HER IDEA.

Let me back up a minute. My baby sister has never expressed the slightest interest in things glue-and-ephemera related. While I was cutting and pasting photos of Harrison Ford and Shawn

Cassidy into my teeny-bopper scrapbooks, she was busy shooting hoops and practicing her overhand volleyball serve. In high school, while I was perfecting my calligraphy and bubble letters, Mindy was heading out to see Iggy Pop in concert at the Warfield in San Francisco.

Over the years, when I'd show her my latest creations, she'd express polite interest, but I was more likely to get her to commit to attending a vacation time-share presentation than to accompany me to a craft night.

That is, until she had a child.

Suddenly, Mindy and her husband owned more cameras than George Lucas. The pictures began pouring into their household, their cute white paper envelopes stacking up on end tables and kitchen counters. Something had to be done to save this young family from a lifetime of unscrapped memories.

As a responsible big sister—and a wily scrapbooker—I knew an opportunity when I saw one. Far be it from me to let a member of my own flesh and blood file her precious baby photos away in shoeboxes! I mapped out my strategy and moved in.

First, I began showing her the adorable mini-albums I made for my own family. "And it only took an hour!" I'd chirp, noting the wrinkle that appeared between her eyebrows. I'd bring an assortment of my favorite projects to family gatherings and leave them scattered on the coffee table. I would catch her surreptitiously leafing through the pages with an unmistakable cloud of mommy-guilt hanging in the air above her head. It was working.

I think the turning point came when, at our family Christmas celebration, my husband opened his gift from me—a small album containing a year's worth of pictures of the kids. Tears started to well up in his eyes as he turned to me and said, "This is the best present ever." I saw my sister watching, so I whispered, "That only took an afternoon to make." The look in her eyes told me the trap had been set, baited, and sprung.

My hunch was confirmed when Mindy began to ask where I buy my supplies, what size of album I like the best, and where I get my pictures developed. Although I projected a calm, disinterested demeanor, I was mentally rubbing my hands together and cackling with glee. She was sunk.

The next time I taught at my local scrapbook store, I called her. "I'm not sure we have enough people to keep the class on the schedule," I told her, a little catch in my voice. "They may cancel it if I don't come up with some more students. Do you think you could come? Please?" She agreed, provided that I show her the difference between a scoring and a cutting blade. "No problem," I said.

The rest, as they say, is history. For Christmas I compiled a scrapbooking care package for her, complete with her own Fiskars trimmer and a subscription to *Simple Scrapbooks* magazine. So I wasn't too shocked when she called me and told me we needed to schedule some scrapbooking time. I did, however, almost choke on my latte when she said she needed to get "caught up." Apparently, I left a few things out of my covert Intro to Scrapbooking Class. Like the fact that you never, ever (EVER!) get "caught up."

Oh well. There are some things a scrapper needs to find out on her own.

SEVENTEEN

On the Run

I've always longed for the mindset of a runner, for the exultation and freedom that supposedly result from hours of grueling training—to say nothing of the runner's body: trim torso, tight abs, long lean legs that look great in flashy Lycra tights. But despite my past attempts, including training for and running two half-marathons (which counts as a *whole* marathon in my book), the only "runner's high" I've experienced has come from oxygen depletion.

Nonetheless, something has drawn me to running lately. And after a few weeks of "training" (5 minutes of running and 15 of walking, doubled over, hand on side, trying to catch my breath), things have gotten a little bit easier. In fact, as I headed out this morning, my steps were sure and my legs strong. My heart raced, but in a good way, and my breath was even! I was flying! For once, I felt like a runner!

Then I turned off my driveway and onto the street. By the time I passed the second house on the left, my breath became ragged, my legs began to protest, and I had to wonder—why do people run? I mean, there have got to be a million other forms of exercise that aren't quite so—shall we say—torturous? But the biggest problem with running, I realized, is not the pain, it's the fact that you cannot scrapbook while you're doing it.

I got to thinking. There have to be some sports that actually enhance my paper-crafting talents. While I might not be able to scrapbook and cross-country ski simultaneously, at least my scrapbooking skills might be refined in some way by my athletic endeavors.

So then I thought, if I'm interested in scrapbooking-friendly physical activities, other people might be, too! Thus, I present to you a list of sports that complement your scrapbook addiction:

1. Golf. I've always been one to think that golf was for old people. Who else would want to watch such a slow-moving spectacle? But now my opinion has changed. Not only can you increase your grip strength (which will pay off the next time you pull out your punches), you can also work on your nature photography while awaiting your turn at the tee. And, if you're really ambitious, you can stash a few page kits in your golf bag to work on between holes. (You may have to leave some of your clubs behind to maximize the space, but no one uses the 4-iron anyway.)

2. Fly fishing. As with golf, there's plenty of downtime to take advantage of, and tons of photo ops. You can also tuck a few embellishments in the empty spots in your tackle box. A filleting knife could, with proper training, be used instead of a craft knife to crop photos and papers. Word of warning—make sure everything you bring with you is waterproof, and keep your rhinestone brads away from the water. Little fishies love sparkly things.

3. Ping pong. The hand-eye coordination you'll gain from playing this fast-moving game is sure to benefit you in applying precision rub-ons or hand-stitching borders on your pages. Plus, the ping-pong table is a great surface for spreading out your work when you're not playing. In fact, with proper positioning of supplies and tools, you could easily take over the entire table for your crafting purposes in no time at all. The kids can go play on the neighbor's table.

4. Bowling. I prefer the old-fashioned, non-computerized lanes, where you keep score using a transparency and a dry-erase pen. That way, you can substitute a SlickWriter for the erasable pen and sneak in a little journaling while you're supposed to be counting strikes and spares. But even if you go to a modern, high-tech bowling alley, you can use the time between turns to sort photos, sketch layouts, and catch up on your idea-book reading.

Hopefully these hints will help you successfully combine your exercising with your crafting. The better shape you're in physically, the more stamina you'll have for your next all-night crop.

EIGHTEEN

The Scrapper's Diet

Like most American women—more than two-thirds, according to some surveys—I'd like to lose a little weight. While 15 or 20 pounds would be awesome, I'd settle for 10. Or 5. Or even just a couple. Oh, heck, let's face it—if I could just lose a few ounces under my double chin, I'd be a happy gal!

I know that slimmer people live longer, feel stronger, and look better. But it's not from lack of trying that I've been unable to shed the baby pounds that have hung on long after my third child entered toddlerhood.

No matter what type of diet I try—and I've tried them all—I'm never able to achieve much success. The cabbage diet stunk up the house so badly that we had to relocate for a day while the kitchen aired out. The protein diet made my skin break out for the first time in years. SlimFast shakes gave me gas.

And on my first day of trying Weight Watchers, I used all of my daily points on a bag of tortilla chips, rationalizing that I could merely shave one point off each daily total for the next month to even it all out. It didn't work.

From the conversations I overhear at the gym, in Nordstrom's dressing room, and among my friends, I am not alone. A lot of thirty-something (okay, almost forty-something) women find it hard to lose weight and get back to their former glory. In fact, the only thing that seems to really work is the old advice about burning off more calories than you consume. Overnight crash diets just won't cut it.

I figured that I might be more likely to actually stick to the plan if I tied it into my favorite hobby. So to aid my fellow suffering scrapbooking sisters, I've adapted a few tried-and-true diet rules to scrapbookers:

1. **Eat a balanced diet.** This means eating a healthy breakfast, lunch, and dinner, plus a few nutritious snacks. This does not mean you eat equally from each of the candy dishes on each of the tables while at your weekly crop.

2. **Get regular exercise.** Trust me; walking from

the couch to the refrigerator won't do it. Neither will browsing the aisles of the local scrapbook store. But, if you find yourself sprinting toward the latest rack of Martha Stewart paper-crafting goods, or engaging in hand-to-hand combat with another scrapper over the last copy of the new Cathy Zielske book, then you can give yourself one exercise point. Likewise, if your scrapbooking tote weighs more than 50 pounds, give yourself credit for strength training each time you load it in and out of the car.

3. If you feel like snacking, start scrapbooking instead. Scrapbooking works for staving off my late-afternoon munchies, because when I've spent an hour on a layout, the last thing I want to do is embellish it with brownie crumbs or chocolate fingerprints. You can't scrap and eat at the same time—at least, not unless you're passionate about the "distressed" look.

4. Reward yourself for your successes. If you stick with your diet for a week, treat yourself to that new set of acrylic stamps. If you stick with your diet for a month, you deserve a new alphabet die set for your Sizzix or QuicKutz. If you reach your target weight, sign up for that scrapbooking retreat in Paris that you've been dying to attend. (Tell your husband I said it was okay.)

5. When all else fails, pull out the secret weapon. Let's face it, even with this plan in place, most of us aren't really going to be able to fit into our pre-baby jeans. So here's a surefire way to lose 5, 10, 20 pounds or more, in just a few hours: clean out your scrap room. Hey, 50 sheets of cardstock weighs about a pound; toss in a few pairs of scissors, a bunch of half-used sticker sheets, and some wood-mounted rubber stamps, and you'll be rid of 10 pounds in no time. There—don't you feel lighter already?

NINETEEN

Head of the Class

Teaching a class at my local scrapbook store seemed like a good idea at the time. I mean, how hard could it be? I've been a scrapbooker for more than a decade, and I've taught all kinds of other classes, from writing to aerobics to Sunday School. This was going to be a walk in the park...or so I thought.

Let me start by saying that teaching scrapbooking is like teaching nothing else on the face of this earth, except maybe open heart surgery. That sounds facetious and overblown, I know, but think about it—what do people feel more strongly about than their memories? Not much, other than their vital organs. And if you put yourself in the position of helping them define, crop, and spatter paint on those memories, you're in for a challenge.

The good thing about scrapbooking is that it's voluntary. Teaching a scrapbooking class is not, for example, like teaching traffic school or high school civics. People are there because they actually want to be—or so you'd assume.

Usually, the students in my classes are pure joy. Well, maybe "pure" is too strong a word. Let me put it this way: despite the occasional challenge, I'd still rather teach a class of six-year-olds how to use foam stamps and acrylic paint than...well, than get a root canal. Or go shopping at Victoria's Secret with my 20-pounds-lighter, 6-inches-taller, 3-years-younger sister.

Teaching—even teaching something I love as much as scrapbooking—is not an easy job. And since many of you may be harboring a secret dream of teaching a class of your own, I've put together a few tips to help you live through the process.

1. There's One in Every Crowd. Despite the opt-in/opt-out nature of the hobby, there are always a few people in every group who look like they had a choice between working on a roadside trash crew or attending a two-hour class on photography for scrapbookers—and the highway litter detail was full. But I'm an optimist: I choose to believe that the woman who threatened to sue me if I trimmed away even a millimeter of her mother's hair from a priceless heritage photo was simply having a bad day.

2. Be a Miser. You know how your kindergarten teacher, Miss Patty, used to pass out just *one* blue piece of construction paper and just *one* yellow piece when it was time for art? Well, there's a reason for that. Humans—and scrappers in particular—tend to hoard things. If we see six pieces of ribbon, we *want* six pieces of ribbon, even if five of them belong to the other students in the class. As a teacher, if you put out a bag of 200 buttons, rest assured that your class will *use* the whole bag of 200 buttons. And since the wages for scrapbook teachers come out to roughly 73 cents an hour, you'll want to keep close tabs on your supplies.

3. Start Small. And I mean "small" as in "kid-sized." After teaching dozens of classes, I can say with complete conviction that children are much easier to handle than adults. First, the kids are easy to please. Give them a glue stick and a jar of glitter, and they're good for half an hour. Second, they're always happy to be there. I've yet to meet a truly grumpy child. Third, if you run out of things to do before class is over, you can always fold cardstock in half and tell them to "make cards." And finally, if they start acting up and getting on your nerves, you can threaten them. That doesn't work with adults.

Teaching is certainly not for everyone. It's incredible to me that many of the top-name scrapbookers fly around the country—and the world—teaching class after class, answering the same questions over and over. Yet they show up each and every time, fresh and ready to give it their all. The next time I get the chance, I'm going to have to sit down with one of them and ask if she's ever been sued...

TWENTY

Scrapbooking Man-to-Man

After trying to explain to my husband for the thousandth time, in terms he'd understand, exactly *why* I find it necessary to spend a good deal of our disposable income and a great deal of my disposable time on paper-related goods and activities, I finally set out to determine what the deal is with men and scrapbooking.

I mean, what's so hard for them to understand? And why don't more of them partake in the hobby? After all, I know more than one "grown-up" guy who spends hours designing model railroads, painting little cars, or playing with radio-controlled airplanes. But they just don't get the scrapbooking thing.

In fact, at a recent Creating Keepsakes Convention, I saw only two men among the hordes of females careening by our table in the make-and-take ballroom. One of them was assisting his elderly mother and appeared to be concentrating on keeping himself from bolting out the door and into the nearest sports bar. And while the other male was totally into it, wielding a tape runner like a true professional, he was definitely in the minority. Most men I know—at least the ones I'm related to—think a trip to a scrapbook store is about as painful as an afternoon on the labor and delivery floor in the local hospital. There's something about scrapbooking that makes them feel like their manhood is being challenged.

I think it's all in the marketing. Here's what I mean. There's nothing inherently "female" or "male" about scrapbooking. In fact, if the paper arts industry wants to draw more testosterone, they only need to incorporate a few simple changes:

1. Power Tools. The Fiskars Craft Drill is a good start, but let's face it. Men like things big, noisy, and heavy—not cute, small, and lightweight. If you told them that your next scrapbook project called for a 125-lb. jackhammer and a "manly man" to operate it, they'd be all over it. And the cute new pastel tools, while appealing to those of us who like to color-coordinate our scissors with our scrapbooking supplies, don't fit the male perception that tools come in two color schemes: DeWalt black-and-gold or John Deere yellow-and-green. Maybe instead of thinking "trendy," scrapbook tool manufacturers should think "sporty," and offer rulers and paper piercers in the colors of the Major League Baseball teams, complete with logos. What man could resist a blue-and-white eyelet setter branded with the New York Yankees logo?

2. Competition. And speaking of sports, you know it's true: men get a rush from competing against—and hopefully beating—their fellow man. Make scrapbooking a competitive sport (maybe by awarding points based on the number of embellishments used or the fastest finishing time), and they'll be right there, organizing three-on-three weekend tournaments. They'll slap each others' rears in congratulatory ecstasy when a particularly difficult technique is mastered, and they'll take frequent breaks to swill Gatorade and (I hate to say it) spit. Jock straps would be optional, but a bullpen is a must.

3. Danger. Right now, the most dangerous thing that can happen while scrapbooking is suffering a nicked finger while trimming ribbon with a pair of super-sharp paper snips. But if we'd just take the guards off the guillotine-style paper cutters and put Surgeon General's Warning labels on our stocks of Diamond Glaze and Mod Podge, our better halves would suddenly see scrapping as an extreme sport, and they'd long to take part.

But wait. After devising these suggestions, a larger question occurred to me—why, exactly, do we *want* men to participate in scrapbooking? In fact, just as I don't want my husband messing around in my kitchen, using up my special stocks of saffron and imported vanilla, I also don't want him pawing my stash of Making Memories and Autumn Leaves. So, let's just forget this whole conversation and pretend I never said anything. The next time my husband asks me why I spend so much time and money on scrapbooking, I'll just shrug, give him a sweet smile and say, "It's a girl thing. You boys just wouldn't understand." And then I'll smack him on the rear.

Stashbusters Anonymous

There's an annual scrapbooking ritual I want to tell you about. Apparently, this is how it goes: wake up one morning in January with your head resting on a box of Sizzix alphabet dies (where your pillow used to be), and suddenly realize that maybe it's not quite, well, *normal* to live like this. Most people don't use their ice-cube trays for housing color-coded embellishments, or store their patterned paper (sorted by manufacturer, of course) in their dishwasher.

Most people have a life outside scrapbook supplies—dull and humdrum as that life may be.

When you come to the realization that your stash might have gotten out of hand, you then decide that for the next 12 months you will bust your behind using it all up. Or, in more common parlance, you'll spend the next year "stashbusting."

I'm all for that! After all, the more I use, the more space I have, and the more space I have, the better excuse I have to go shopping for additional supplies. As I've gathered from my research, you're supposed to come up with some guidelines or rules to follow for your stashbusting efforts, just so things are perfectly clear before you start. For instance, you might decide that you can buy additional cardstock, but no patterned paper. Or you can purchase items you need to complete an assigned project, but self-made assignments don't count.

So here are my rules for the stashbusting year ahead. For the next 12 months, I commit to not buying a single scrapbooking item, with the following exceptions:

1. Items I must purchase in order to complete a project that I started before my stashbusting pledge are exempt. These items include, but are not limited to, my annual album, my wedding album, my children's "School of Life" albums, and my "Library of Memories" albums.

2. Items I must purchase in order to complete
   a paying assignment are exempt. These
   items include, but are not limited to, layouts
   for magazines, layouts I am thinking about
   submitting to magazines, and layouts I am not
   now considering submitting to magazines, but
   may submit at some time in the future.

3. Items I must purchase as supplies for classes
   or workshops are exempt. These items include,
   but are not limited to, classes or workshops
   I am taking or thinking about taking, and
   classes or workshops I am teaching or thinking
   about teaching.

4. Items purchased at stores that are going out
   of business are exempt. These items include,
   but are not limited to, fixtures, equipment,
   carpeting, etc.

5. Items purchased to make a gift for friends and/
   or family are exempt. These items include, but
   are not limited to, cards, calendars, notebooks,
   albums, mini-cards, mini-notebooks, mini-
   calendars, and mini-albums.

6. Items purchased at a discount of at least 30 percent are exempt (tax excluded).

7. Items purchased while on vacation are exempt.

8. Items purchased while under self-induced duress (e.g., "You MUST have that QuicKutz font. Buy it. Buy it NOW!") are exempt.

9. Items that are, or potentially may be, discontinued are exempt.

10. Items that are pink or polka-dotted are exempt.

11. Items that include the words "As seen at winter CHA" are exempt.

12. Items that are or may become collectors' items are exempt.

13. Items purchased with another use in mind but that somehow ended up in my scrap space are exempt. These items include, but are not limited to, scissors, lunchboxes, paint cans, thread, etc.

14. Items purchased with a giftcard are exempt.

15. Purchases of craft store giftcards are exempt.

16. Items purchased with PayPal funds are exempt.

17. Items purchased for, or received from, swaps are exempt.

18. Items I do not remember purchasing are exempt.

19. Items purchased to replace a used-up, lost, or otherwise missing original are exempt.

20. Items I bought on impulse and then ended up not using are exempt.

21. Items recommended by a "scrap celebrity" are exempt. These items include, but are not limited to, those sold on QVC and the Aveeno lotion that Cathy Zielske swears by.

There. I think that's sufficiently restrictive. I feel better already.

Now that I've got that out of my system, who wants to go shopping?

{ TWENTY-TWO }

Coming Out of the Closet

The biggest obstacle for a scrapbooker isn't finding an efficient and eye-pleasing way to store forty-seven colors of cardstock. It isn't locating the latest Heidi Swapp Bling the day after its release. And it isn't even deciding whether you should enter the *Memory Makers* Masters, *Creating Keepsakes* Hall of Fame, or Scrapbooker of the Year contests. The single biggest challenge facing today's scrapbookers is introducing your friends and families to your secret life of scrapbooking.

It may sound like a little thing. After all, what's the big deal? In the latest polls, almost a third of all American households contain a family member who participates in scrapbooking at some level. That's more people than watched the season finale of *American Idol*!

But still, when you tell people you scrapbook,

you get one of the following three responses:

1. The "Huh?" People who give you the "Huh?" honestly have no idea what you are talking about. Mention scrapbooking, and their minds automatically go to the black paper-and-pressboard albums their grandmothers diligently created, complete with paste-on photo corners and crackling black-and-white photos. These people—typically computer engineers and typically male—consider scrapbooking to be about as modern as milk delivered to your doorstep in glass bottles, non-HDTV, and 256-MB pre-Intel computer processors. Usually, the next question after the initial "Huh?" is "Why?" Forget about winning this group over unless you're a digital scrapbooker; then all you have to do is show them your latest Photoshop creation and watch as their "???" turn to "!!!"

2. The "Uh-Huh." This snide response (usually accompanied by a smirk) comes from those sadly misinformed souls who think they know "all about" scrapbooking. They equate the hobby with high-pressure house parties, kitschy appliquéd sweatshirts, and dozens of cats. These know-it-alls will slowly back away from you after you've told them of your passion, and they will likely avoid all contact with you for the remainder of your life, for fear that: A. Scrapbooking is a contagious, life-threatening disease, or B. You will force a pair of scissors into their hands and make them crop all their precious heritage photos into heart shapes. The solution? Hand them the latest edition of your favorite scrapbook magazine or email them the link to Elsie Flannigan's blog and leave them alone. Don't be surprised if you see them at the local scrapbook store the next week, stocking up on cardstock and 7gypsies 97% Complete journaling tags.

3. The "Yippee!" As you may have guessed, this yodel of excitement is the response you'll receive when you've located one of your own. Just as an ex-pat from Lichtenstein would be thrilled to discover a fellow countryman on a desert isle in the Caribbean, so we greet our like-minded hobbyists. Once the common language is confirmed, conversation will quickly turn to detailed discussions of page sizes and preferred styles. Sports fans bond over a dissection of recent trades and pennant races; scrapbookers bond through an analysis of which cardstock texture is best for hand-journaling, and whether manufacturers will *ever* create a "self-adhesive" chipboard that is truly self-adhesive. Upon parting ways, you both recognize that you may never encounter each other again, but you will also acknowledge that you've been somehow enriched by the experience, whether through a recommended online source for Daisy D's closeouts or a new trick for resizing photos in Photoshop Elements.

The number of people who fall into the first two categories seems far larger than what the statistics indicate we should encounter. Maybe the numbers lie, or maybe we scrapbookers are all locked away in our private cubbies, Dotto adhesive rollers in hand. I have another explanation: I think scrapbookers are running around in the general population, hiding our photo-preservation proclivities in the closet for fear of repercussion once the word is out. There's only one remedy for this fear: we need to proclaim our preferences loudly, perhaps by prominently pinning a "Out and Proud Scrapbooker" ribbon (made of polka-dot grosgrain, of course) to our Crop-in-Style totes. We need to let the rest of society know that we're just like them—we just have larger paper collections. We have nothing to be embarrassed of. After all, it's not like we're *quilters* or something.

TWENTY-THREE

Those Poor Kids

I t can't be easy to be the child of a scrapbooker. I'm the first say that I feel sympathy for the hundreds of children whose mothers missed yet another bedtime story because they had to finish "just one more layout." Who were forced to subsist on PB&J sandwiches and Goldfish Crackers for weeks on end because Mommy spent the grocery money on Doodlebug ribbon instead of Hamburger Helper. Who went to school with broken Crayolas and dried-up markers because their moms earmarked the "good" school supplies for themselves.

Sure, these are extreme examples, the exceptions rather than the rule. Most scrappers' kids do get plenty of snuggles, nutritious food, and ample amounts of crayons and construction paper. But the fact is, it's still not easy to be the kid of a scrapbooker. And the reason has nothing to do with neglectful parenting—in fact, it's the opposite. Scrapbookers' kids never get a moment to themselves. Instead, they've got photographic documentation of every stumble, every misstep, and every humiliating minute.

Forget the embarrassing photos of the naked baby on the bearskin rug: that's nothing. Like little divas and dukes, scrappers' kids live their lives in the limelight, facing the flash of the paparazzi at every turn. The time little Sally ran through the house with a bathroom plunger in hand, wearing only a colander on her head? Mom got it. The time cute Joey smeared his body with chocolate pudding and did the Macarena on the dining room table? Yep. It's all there in black and white, sepia, and full-color—enlarged and digitally enhanced, too.

Sometimes it's not the photos, but the actual taking of the photos, that is so darned embarrassing. Like when Mom insisted on climbing aboard the bus to get the traditional first-day-of-school photos...which would have been okay if the child in question had been starting first grade, not tenth. Or when Mommy Dearest met her son at Hong's Chinese Restaurant on his first date not only to take photos, but to grab the fortune from his cookie for the scrapbook page as well. Fast-forward to the honeymoon and it's easy to see why elopement is beginning to sound like an attractive option for kids whose moms live with their Canons in hand.

Even when photographic proof of those embarrassing moments is unavailable, scrapbooking moms still manage to document the events. They carry little journals everywhere they go, jotting down notes just in case their elephantine memories somehow fail them. They know exactly when Bobby first "made doo-doo" in the big boy toilet. They can tell you what color underwear Kendall wore to preschool graduation. They know not only at what age Cassie got her first bra, but exactly what size it was—and they may have the actual garment itself on display in the scrapbook, in all its 32AAA glory.

And if the scrapbook page weren't enough, sometimes they insist on posting their kids' most excruciatingly humiliating life events on the Internet, for the entire WORLD to gawk at, review, and comment on. Activists worldwide are up in arms because the Internet has become a haven for gambling, pornography, and other vices, and we have parental controls, spam blockers, and spyware protection to deal with the onslaught. But the real question is, can anything be done about those online scrapbooking forums where moms gather to exchange tales of filial embarrassment?

There's no easy solution. Perhaps a warning on scrapbooking websites? Maybe an album-rating standard, where scrapbookers must indicate the level of potential embarrassment to family members their projects hold? What about a surcharge on the sale of acid-free products, where all proceeds are set aside to fund future therapy for the children of scrapbookers? Or maybe the best solution is also the easiest. All scrapbookers' kids should internalize their wounds, letting them fester, as they mature into adulthood. Then, they can do unto others what's been done unto them. They can begin scrapbooking, highlighting all their *parents'* most embarrassing moments, posting the results on the Internet for all to see.

After all, turnabout is fair play.

TWENTY-FOUR

I'm Good Enough, I'm Smart Enough...

There's an interesting phenomenon I've noticed with scrapbooking. Well, there are several interesting phenomena (after all, that's why I'm writing this book). But this particular one has to do with motivation.

As scrapbookers, we usually begin documenting our family's history to leave a legacy for the future. We want our kids—and our kids' kids—to know more than just what we looked like. We want them to know what we thought about, what our daily lives were like, and that at one point in our lives we owned over 40 pairs of shoes (20 of them black). We want them to see the real *us*. We also want to have a record of our lives in case we end up like the old lady in *The Notebook* and need to be reminded of who we were, once our kids (yes, the same ones whose first steps we noted so carefully in our scrapbooks) shut us up in the senior citizens' home.

While our initial reasons are generally altruistic, sometimes things change. Somewhere around the stage where we spend more time reading the latest issues of our scrapbooking magazines than we do reading the daily newspaper, our goals may shift. For some of us, our scrapbooking starts to be less about our family and more about—well, I'll come right out and say it—getting published.

Many a scrapper I've known has reached a point where she wants public recognition for her work. Instead of, "Oh, I hope little Taylor appreciates all the time and effort I put into her book," it becomes, "Taylor! Get your hands off that page! I have to send it in to the *Simple Scrapbooks* call for layouts tomorrow, and if you get dirty fingerprints on it, so help me, I'm going to make you spend your weekend sorting my patterned paper by manufacturer, and then you'll be sorry!"

Why would we move from scrapping for our families to scrapping in hopes of finding fame and fortune—or at least a few free product samples? The answer is pretty simple. It's all about validation.

So much in our lives can be thankless, behind-the-scenes, or downright invisible. No one calls us on the phone to tell us how inspiring we were as we changed the sheets. No company sponsors an award for the woman who drives the most carpool miles. No one wants our autograph or asks us where we get our inspiration because we've done such a great job cleaning dishes, wiping heinies, or checking homework papers. It can feel like we're taken for granted. So when we realize there's recognition available for our scrapbook pages, it's like a beam of light shines down, illuminating our upturned faces and shiny sinks (or in my case, full-of-dirty-dishes sink).

Sometimes, we convince ourselves that publication will set things right (and sometimes it sounds much easier than convincing our husbands or children to pitch in a bit more...). Seeing our page in a magazine means something. It means someone else (besides our husband, kids, and mother) thinks our photography was good enough, our journaling was "smart" enough, and our color selections were slick enough. But publication isn't just a validation of our skills with paper and ink: it means our kids are cute, our lives are meaningful, and, gosh darn it, people *like* us!

Once we've been published, it doesn't matter if there are crackers under the car seats or dog hairs permanently adhered to the couch. We've already grabbed the golden ring. We're "CK-OK." We can go back to the dishes and the laundry and the carpool knowing that, at least in one area, we've passed the test. It's also useful justification to our significant others that all those hours spent slicing and embellishing at the dining room table were important. Publication is the scrapper's equivalent of the Cooperstown Baseball Hall of Fame, except without the cool uniforms.

And that, my friends, a memory worth keeping.

{ TWENTY-FIVE }

Can I Have Your Autograph?

I never thought I'd be a celebrity stalker. I made it through my teen years with only a minor crush on Shawn Cassidy. In college, as a campus tour guide, I led Sigourney Weaver around the grounds without blinking an eye—or asking for her autograph. I just wasn't the type of girl to devour Hollywood gossip or be impressed by fame and fortune.

And then I became a scrapbooker. And suddenly, I'm following my favorite stars with more dogged determination than a paparazzi photographer hot on the trail of a Jolie/Pitt sighting. The only difference is my prey isn't an A-list, tinsel-town celebrity; I'm after the stars of the scrapbooking world.

First, I fell in scrapping love with Becky Higgins. Like a junior high girl modeling herself after the coolest twelfth-grader around, I mooned after

Becky. She was the epitome of the girl next door, except better—she had a cool job, too!

Then came Heidi Swapp. Talk about glamour—this gal has it oozing from her pores! More than once, I've taken a picture of the Swappalicious into the hair salon and told my stylist, "Make me look like this." (And, I should tell you, more than once my stylist has gently patted my shoulder and told me, "In your dreams, honey, in your dreams.")

Not long after my infatuation with The Swappster, my horizons grew broader. Onto the scene came Ali Edwards, Cathy Zielske, Donna Downey, and Stacy Julian. I began to study all these women, hoping to find the secrets to their success, style, and stardom. But the list didn't stop there.

Each year when the *Creating Keepsakes* Hall of Fame winners were announced, I'd have a new crop of starlets to choose from. I'd comb through the winners with all the attention of a frat boy scanning the incoming freshman girls, rating their potential and predicting their fame quotient. Who will be asked to author a book, create a font, launch a product line? Who will teach at Creating Keepsakes University? Who will be the next "overnight success?"

I'm not alone in my adoration of the superstars of the scrapping world. These women can't come within 50 yards of a scrapbook store without some desperate scrapper asking them to bless their photo trimmer or give them advice on picture placement. The stars themselves don't seem to understand the attraction. "I'm just a regular gal," they all claim modestly.

But as much as they say they're just "normal people," we know that's not true. After all, "normal people" don't receive scads of free product delivered right to their doors on a regular basis, so much free product, in fact, that they are forced to GIVE AWAY perfectly good stuff to undeserving folks like their mothers.

"Normal people" don't have strangers stopping them in the grocery store, asking them to sign their "I LIVE TO SCRAP" t-shirts.

Speaking of shirts, "normal people" don't have their own lines of clothing and accessories emblazoned with their catch phrases.

"Normal people" aren't greeted by hundreds of screaming women (some of whom are dressed up in wigs, glasses, and clothing to *look* like them) when they enter a room at a convention to teach.

These scrap goddesses really need to face the facts: there's nothing normal about them. Not only are they making a living at the thing we scrappers are so passionate about, not only are they jetting across the country and around the world, bringing the message of memory-keeping to all they encounter, there's also the fact that *there is not an ugly one among them.*

I'm serious—look at these gals. They're gorgeous! They radiate life; they shine with enthusiasm; they glow. What I want to know is, which came first, the scrapping or the aura? In other words, did they rise through the ranks of scrapping *because* they are so cute, or did they become cute as a result of scrapping?

I think I know the answer to this one, but I hold out hope that if I go through enough Hermafix and American Crafts ribbon, I, too, will have perfectly waved blond hair and an adorable smile.

I can dream, can't I?

About the Author

When she created her first layout over a decade ago, Lain fell head-over-heels in love with scrapbooking—and thus her obsession with words, paper, and glue sticks began. She soon figured out she needed to make a living by scrapbooking or she was going to have trouble justifying her patterned paper purchases to her usually understanding husband, John. A contributing editor to *Simple Scrapbooks* magazine, Lain entertains scrapbookers worldwide through her blog, (*getscraphappy.com*), scrapbooking podcasts, and in-person and online classes. When not scrapping, Lain is an obsessed crafter, crossword fanatic, and dedicated Little League mom. She lives with her family and scrapbooking stash in Northern California.

About Simple Scrapbooks *magazine*

For the past 7 years and counting, *Simple Scrapbooks* magazine has been inspiring readers worldwide, giving them the knowledge, tools, and confidence they need to fit scrapbooking into their busy lives. Through a successful bi-monthly magazine, top-selling special issues and books, and an interactive online community, *Simple Scrapbooks* helps its readers keep their scrapbook projects simple, meaningful, and above all, fun!

simplescrapbooksmag.com

Simple
Scrapbooks™

Founding Editor
Stacy Julian

Editor in Chief
Jennafer Martin

Managing Editor
Angie Lucas

Creative Editor
Wendy Smedley

Senior Editor
Megan Hoeppner

Copy Editor
Jenny Webb

Editorial Assistant
Carolyn Jolley

Art Director
Cathy Zielske

Illustration
Teri Dimalanta

CK MEDIA

ISBN 1-934176-18-4